1 INTRODUCTION

DEFINING NETWORKING

To some, networking means simply meeting or calling someone new for what might be a one-off discussion or event. In this limited sense, networking is only a trading relationship in which two parties seek to discover whether they have anything of mutual interest to talk about. They either make some sort of exchange or quickly move on. This makes networking a highly 'transactional' subject, much like buying and selling or negotiating with someone.

Our very different view in this book is that networking has a much wider definition. In fact, it can be a major social and life skill to be used in both a business/organisational and a personal setting.

NETWORK & RELATIONSHIP BUILDING

The 'relationship building' aspect of networking is a long-term commitment to knowing more about yourself and others, and what you may be able to do together that you couldn't do (or couldn't do as well) alone.

We will, therefore, focus on how anyone can systematically adopt effective networking as an individual strategy. We will consider how it can play a key part in linking you with a wider range of people who can help you to achieve more – **whatever 'more' means for you.**

INTRODUCTION

BENEFITS OF NETWORKING

The benefits of effective networking are many. Some of these are:

- It is the most **cost effective** marketing tool available
- Networking referrals will typically generate **80% more results** than a cold call
- **70-80% of all jobs** are found through networking
- Every person you meet has **200-250 people with whom they connect** who can potentially assist you
- **Anyone** that you might want to meet or contact **in the world**, is only **five to six people contacts** away from you

BENEFITS OF NETWORKING

As if these reasons were not enough, a healthy and active link to a network is a vast resource available to every individual at a low personal cost. It can help you to achieve a range of goals that otherwise might be too hard or out of reach.

A key point to understand is that networking is achieved at **low** personal cost <u>not</u> **no** personal cost. We are not suggesting that networking is a quick fix or *fad* idea that can be easily adopted to make things better for a while. However, it can provide immediate results for those prepared to invest their time and energy.

FOUR STAGES

In this book, our effective networking and relationship building journey will be taken in four stages or steps. These are:

If you commit the first letters of each of the four stages to memory, it spells the easy-to-remember word **LINK**. Linking people successfully is what networking is all about.

CONCEPT OF NETWORKING

Many of the definitions of networking
shown on the next page may
surprise some people, in as much
as they suggest that networking
is an altruistic activity involving
giving and sharing, rather
than taking.

NETWORKING DEFINITIONS

- A power that comes from a spirit of giving and sharing
- A willingness to honour ourselves, our relationships and our connections with the universal flow
- A way of sending out into the system what we have and what we know, and having it return to re-circulate continually through the network
- An organised way of creating links from people we know to people they know for a specific purpose
- Giving, contributing to and supporting others without keeping score
- People caring about people
- Fostering self-help, and the exchange of information; seeking to change society and work life and to share resources
- Ensuring the right to ask a favour without hooks

THE LEARNING STAGE

INTRODUCTION

The Learning Stage focuses on how individuals who want to network go about understanding their own personal style and their goals or aims from networking.

It then looks at what is involved in positive and effective networking (as opposed to poor networking practice) and where to begin the journey.

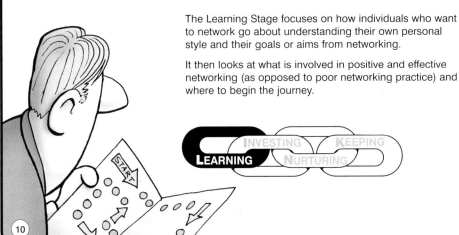

1: LEARNING STAGE

YOUR PERSONAL NEEDS

Before you even begin to look at engaging seriously in lots of networking effort, it is useful to look at your own *temperament* or *disposition*. This is the individual's internal desire to network and to find value and enjoyment from the whole process of building relationships.

For some people this will be an almost irrelevant issue to debate. Their motivation to want to talk to people regularly and to network is naturally high. Talking to strangers in supermarket queues, at bus/train stops or even in the elevators is characteristic of such people. However, even if you really enjoy talking to people, it is a proven fact that most of us are not highly confident and highly motivated networkers. In fact, statistics reveal that:

**Only one in ten people is actually comfortable in striking
up a relationship with a complete stranger**

Unfortunately, this means that their own misgivings, fears and doubts potentially hinder the vast majority of people.

1: LEARNING STAGE

FOUR NETWORKING TYPES

In practice, you can divide people who attempt to build networking relationships into four distinct *types*.

The four networking types:

1. Loner (little or no networking)
2. Socialiser
3. User
4. Relationship Builder or Networker

Although our aim is to consider the fourth of these in some detail as the role to which we can all aspire (if we are not already there), let's briefly look at each of these types in turn.

LONER

- Likes to do most things by himself (because he does it faster or best)

- Doesn't want to bother or worry other people

- Feels that his knowledge and skills are often superior to most people

- Only asks for help as a last resort (and when it may be too late)

1: LEARNING STAGE

LONER

The loner is an easily recognisable type, because there are times when we all believe that we will do a job better ourselves than if we ask others for help. The loner will not usually want to bother anyone else, or necessarily see much point in doing so, believing that others will be slower and will set lower standards.

Unfortunately, the loner attitude is a major obstacle to effective networking. We need to shift our thinking greatly in this area. We should be more willing to let others assist, and we should even ask for help more often.

1: LEARNING STAGE

SOCIALISER

- Tries to make a friend of everyone she meets

- Tends to know people's names and faces but not what they do

- Is not usually systematic or ordered about follow-up – contact is random

- May not listen too deeply and is quick to move on

SOCIALISER

Although the socialiser may have a wide circle of friends and contacts, he or she knows little of substance about personal skills and resources. As a result, socialisers do not often share their skills.

The socialiser is also a random networker, following little or no formal contact system.

USER

- Is likely to collect business cards without really connecting with the people

- Tries to make 'sales' or 'pitches' on the first encounter

- Talks and focuses on own agenda rather than to gather information

- Has superficial interactions

- Keeps score when giving favours

USER

Unfortunately, people of this type **do** network widely, but in a way that creates little benefit for themselves or others. Even worse, this kind of networker tends to create a bad impression and therefore can give networking an image of being about selling, taking, bargaining and keeping score.

There is far too much user-led networking, and we will subsequently focus on ways in which this can be avoided.

1: LEARNING STAGE

BUILDER

- Has a 'giving' disposition or *abundance* mentality

- Is generally happy to ask others for help or guidance

- Listens and learns about people carefully

- Is regularly on the look-out for useful information from which others can also benefit

- Has a well-ordered and organised networking system

BUILDER

This type of networker is what this book is all about – an individual who takes a long-term perspective on relationships with others and thinks more about what he or she can give or offer, than about the return.

This type is *out there* for others, or on call to offer help whenever it is needed. If they cannot help in person, they usually know someone else who can.

MAINTAINING HIGH SELF-ESTEEM

Apart from the 'builder', one factor connects the other three types in preventing them from networking more effectively. This is the issue of **self-esteem**.

The **loner** believes in himself or herself, but not necessarily in others (especially relative strangers). The **socialiser** likes people but also very much wants to be liked by others (and therefore does not want to ask for favours). Finally, the **user** takes a relatively selfish view of 'If I benefit or gain, I might reciprocate, otherwise I won't'.

Of course, **all of these types fear either rejection, obligation, being too pushy or even looking weak**. All of these fears or concerns about networking need to be lessened or overcome.

CYCLES OF CONSCIOUSNESS

In a short book such as this, a topic as large and potentially complicated as a person's relative self-esteem cannot be covered at any level of detail. However, it is important to appreciate how low self-esteem can have a major impact on your networking efforts if it is not at least basically understood and addressed.

As the *cycles of consciousness* chart shows on the next page, an individual with high self-esteem is likely to build his own confidence to want to network by having a positive, open and 'can do' attitude.

Conversely, an individual with low self-esteem is likely to lack confidence to start with. She will convince herself (and others) that she has little that would be of interest to others in any network.

POSITIVE CYCLE OF NETWORKING CONSCIOUSNESS

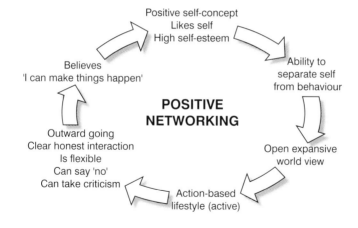

Positive self-concept
Likes self
High self-esteem

Ability to
separate self
from behaviour

POSITIVE NETWORKING

Believes
'I can make things happen'

Outward going
Clear honest interaction
Is flexible
Can say 'no'
Can take criticism

Open expansive
world view

Action-based
lifestyle (active)

1: LEARNING STAGE

NATURE OF NETWORKING

Networking effectiveness starts with a positive personal attitude and an understanding that **successful networking is built on a spirit of giving and sharing and <u>not</u> of bargaining and keeping score.**

Armed with this knowledge, we can now look at how the process of good networking actually works in practice.

The first thing to realise about networking is that everyone you meet is a useful prospective network contact. This seemingly simple fact is often overlooked, as people engage in their own private screening process before they will talk to anyone.

There is obviously a line to be drawn between talking to anyone and everyone in the street and talking to almost no one. However, if you want to network more and to do so successfully, there are many situations that qualify as 'the right opportunity'.

TAKING INTEREST IN ANYBODY & EVERYBODY

It is often the case that we don't really know very much about even close people around us (let alone distant contacts). Even if we do know a little, we are less likely to know how far or deep their skill, knowledge or resources extend. If this is true of your knowledge of others, how much do they really know about you?

Herein lies the basic secret of networking success:

- **You have to become interested in anybody and everybody**
- **You have to share more about yourself than you may have done in the past**

It is out of this mutual exchange of knowledge that network contacts will connect and start to offer support, help, advice, favours, referrals and other benefits on a regular basis.

CORE PROCESSES

Developing a conscious understanding of this *giving and sharing strategy* can take some time and some practice.

In her book 'How to master networking', Robyn Henderson calls this process earning the right to ask a favour of another person, or giving without hooks. Both of these statements imply two processes that operate pretty much at the same time (and neither of them necessarily our first reaction).

The two processes in earning the right to ask a favour are:

- **Giving away information (to be helpful)**
- **Being open for any help you may need**

Let's look at these two processes in turn.

GIVING AWAY INFORMATION

Whether it is accidental or planned, formal or informal, random or structured, in discussion with other people the effective networker offers his or her knowledge, skills, ideas, resources, guidance or data **freely** – without any 'hooks' or expectations that repayment is due in any form. In fact, the only immediate benefit may be the pleasure to be derived from assisting someone with information that was of value to them.

Whilst the giver expects nothing in return, the receiver has a very positive experience and memory of you upon which they can act (if they so choose) in the future. If they do, either directly or indirectly, at some indeterminate time, you **may** receive some reciprocal benefit.

BEING OPEN FOR HELP

Along with openly offering any possible help and support, the effective networker does not operate as a *one-way helper* or *superperson/white knight/angel* coming to the rescue of everyone else, but never personally in need of assistance. He or she also talks realistically about personal goals, tasks, challenges, problems and general issues, and acknowledges feeling vulnerable in not being able to do everything single-handedly.

Being open means being receptive to help when it is offered and, on occasions, asking networking contacts if they can suggest ideas, strategies or approaches that could assist you.

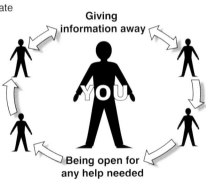

TWO-WAY PROCESS

As the diagram on the previous page illustrates, these two processes operate at the same time and together to create a cycle through which 'favours' are continually offered to all who participate. These favours are both offered and taken in order to keep the network strong and capable of growing to include more and more people.

This process is called 'reciprocity'. It simply means that effective networking is a coin with two sides rather than just one. You can't have one without the other.

Successful networking is therefore about:

- Giving <u>and</u> receiving
- Contributing <u>and</u> accepting support
- Offering <u>and</u> requesting
- Promoting others' needs <u>and</u> promoting your own needs
- Trust <u>and</u> persistence

HOW TO RESEARCH POTENTIAL CONTACTS

We suggested earlier that **every individual in the whole world is potentially only five or six contact steps away.** This 'five or six degrees of separation' shows that even an entire population of over five billion people is still highly accessible.

For practical purposes however, we don't necessarily want or need to meet millions, or even thousands, of people in different organisations, age groups, religions, professions, cultures or places. Ideally therefore, we need some kind of filtering or research system that will help us to build a set of relationships of high quality, or a strong network that can find people and resources both efficiently and effectively.

FIRST STEPS

The first step in the filtering process is to establish what sort of contacts or relationships *you* think may be of value or benefit to you (or the organisation of which you are a part). This is not to run counter to the idea we have been stressing that networking is primarily about giving, but suggests that some relationships are clearly more valuable in the long-term for both sides, given careful thought in the first place. **Only you can determine this 'value'.**

You may already know, or be close to, someone very powerful or influential but gain no benefit from the association. On the other hand, you may find someone in the street where you live who can bring you great benefit if you build a relationship with them. You just need to know what you'd like to achieve in order to make a reasonable assessment.

NETWORKING PYRAMID

When you start to network more widely, you quickly realise that there is a pyramid, or hierarchy of depth or quality in all of your potential relationships. The networking pyramid is shown below.

The networking pyramid

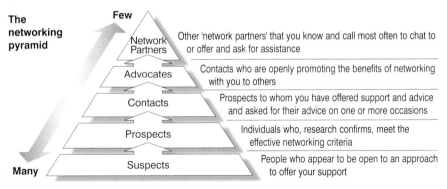

Few

Network Partners — Other 'network partners' that you know and call most often to chat to or offer and ask for assistance

Advocates — Contacts who are openly promoting the benefits of networking with you to others

Contacts — Prospects to whom you have offered support and advice and asked for their advice on one or more occasions

Prospects — Individuals who, research confirms, meet the effective networking criteria

Suspects — People who appear to be open to an approach to offer your support

Many

1: LEARNING STAGE

PYRAMID LEVELS

At the base of the pyramid are what we call '**suspects**'. These are people who seem open to an approach to offer support (remembering our earlier points about giving and reciprocity).

It is usually better to find out more about suspects before approaching them in person. Many are often misidentified and only randomly picked. Only some suspects (when researched more closely) get to the next stage of being 'prospects'.

Prospects are individuals who research confirms meet the effective network criteria, and can usually be approached in person. Once again, initial conversation may reveal that not all prospects have been correctly identified. However, the numbers of people at this level are fewer and you can be much more patient in letting time provide an answer.

PYRAMID LEVELS

Contacts are prospects to whom you have offered support and advice and whose assistance or guidance you have requested on one or more occasions. At this stage, you may have discovered only minor opportunities to call, talk or contact one another, but the potential to do more has been established.

Advocates are contacts who are openly promoting or advocating the benefits of networking (with you in particular) to other prospects and contacts. Although this may not mean frequent contact, it is likely to be more frequent than with general contacts in your network.

Partners are the best and most effective networkers that you know, and the ones you most often call to chat to, to ask advice, or to suggest ideas or options. By this stage, the relationship has generally reached a much higher level of mutual trust and understanding.

USING THE PYRAMID TO LOOK FOR OPPORTUNITIES

To begin to discover who might be your network suspects at the base of the pyramid, an excellent place to start is to *read* for opportunities much more widely.

This means becoming broadly alert to the many opportunities to network that may present themselves every single day. Many of these opportunities will be *posted* in newspapers, magazines, on noticeboards, in advertisements, on the Internet and many other sources.

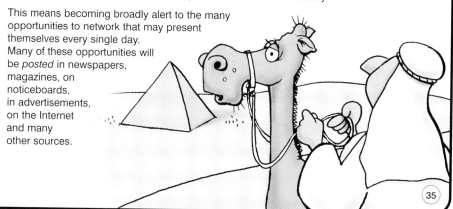

USING THE PYRAMID TO LOOK FOR OPPORTUNITIES

An increased alertness will count for little unless you have a well thought through perspective on what you are looking for. There is no point in networking for the sake of networking. To an extent, this will depend upon your overall personal networking aims and objectives.

Possible networking goals:

- To increase market share/customers
- To find new ideas
- To learn and develop yourself
- To find a job/work/career
- To find new colleagues/friends
- To pursue a hobby or interest
- To gain new perspectives on topics of interest to you
- To go into business for yourself

DIFFERENT KINDS OF NETWORK

Every one of these networking goals is a worthy aim in itself, but it is usually the case that only one or two goals of this type will apply at any one time. Consequently, your networking research efforts will be invested quite differently if your goals are broadly around work or career options rather than if they are about starting up your own business.

Hence, although a few people will have very wide and diverse interests and a broad array of interesting contacts, our networking pyramids are built according to our specific goals and interest areas. This is often why we talk about a *jobs network, a small business network,* an *education network* and so on.

1: LEARNING STAGE

WHERE TO START

So far we have talked about personal motivation, fears and obstacles to networking, and reflecting upon your goals in order to focus your efforts. However, **there is ultimately no better way to start networking than to try it for real**. The easiest way to do this is to commence with the people you already know, rather than to find new ones.

One highly beneficial task you can undertake at the outset is to *map* or chart your contacts. This mapping can be done in a number of ways.

Network Mapping Methods:

- Write a manual list of who you know and what they do
- Build an electronic database of contacts
- Keep a journal or diary of who you meet, where and when
- Draw (and keep updating) a contacts map

MAPPING YOUR NETWORK

Whilst you may eventually choose to adopt two, three or all of these methods, in the early stages it is the last of these options that is often the most helpful and potentially revealing.

A network map is simply drawn (using squares or circles). You start by putting your name in the centre of the page in a circle and commence drawing connecting lines to people you know, before drawing connecting lines from these people to others that they know. A simple example of such a map is shown on the next page.

SIMPLE NETWORK MAP

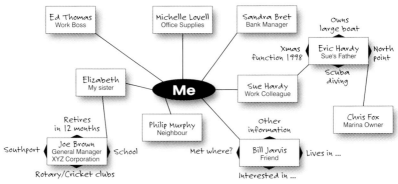

10 categories/groups from which to draw your contacts:			
1. Family	3. Work colleagues	5. Customers	7. Club members	9. Advisers (bank, insurance, etc)
2. Friends	4. Church	6. Suppliers	8. Neighbours	10. School/college/education

MAPPING CONVENTIONS

This very basic map demonstrates how a visual and dynamic chart can be created, which can help both to record quite complex data (and how it is related) and reveal possible avenues that were not obvious before.

One convention (shown for a couple of people in this chart) is recording four pieces of information for every contact in your network (apart from their name). These are their *location*, their *interests, where or how you met* and *any other useful information* that you think is relevant. Whilst this may seem a bit strange and unnecessary for close family and friends, it is remarkable how useful this will be as you build your network over time.

Don't forget, these charts can be used three-dimensionally. When one side or part of it gets too big, transfer a major *hub* name to the centre of another chart and start to use all the new space you now have for extra contacts.

START THE NETWORKING ADVENTURE

Whilst family, friends and other easily identifiable contacts are a good place to start your networking efforts, sooner or later you will need to extend yourself beyond your familiar surroundings and look to attend relevant meetings and/or events.

In many ways, the type of meeting or event that you choose is not particularly important. If your hobby is old model trains, and someone advertises an 'old model train meeting and exhibition' you are obviously likely to meet lots of people who might become good network contacts. However, this is likely to be the exception rather than the rule.

In most cases, meetings or social gatherings of people will be much more general affairs and ones that can only be broadly 'qualified' for their possible relevance.

START THE NETWORKING ADVENTURE

The trick in networking (if there is one) is to **treat all meetings or events as an adventure.**

Like any adventure, you may have some fear and trepidation about facing the unexpected. But you should also feel some of the thrill of the challenge and excitement in finding new people with whom you can really connect.

By making time in your schedule to attend, you can use your early opportunities to watch others networking and to get into the habit of talking to the people you meet.

Don't forget, networking successfully means that we sometimes have to stretch ourselves to the edges of our comfort zones – hard at first but much easier with practice.

BE PREPARED

Whether it is a formal meeting or event (with one hundred people) or an informal gathering (of only ten or less), being ready or open to network is very important – like the Scout's motto 'Be Prepared'.

Even if you are shy, introverted, nervous, bored, or tired, you just never know when you are going to bump into interesting and useful people.

Part of this process of 'being prepared' is to have crisp information about yourself available so that your communication is **short, focused and clear**. Some of this is provided by a good business card (of which we will say more shortly). However, effective networking is rarely achieved by saying 'Hello' and merely handing over a business card – you have also got to give something of yourself as a person.

1: LEARNING STAGE

'SO, WHAT DO YOU DO?'

It pays to think hard about what you could and should communicate in what might be only a few seconds. It is amazing how many people respond to the question 'What do you do?' with 'That's a difficult/interesting question!' or 'I'm an engineer/analyst/administrator/ co-ordinator/manager!'.

Such responses do little to educate the person asking. It is far better to give some pre-thought to this question (even if there are two or three versions of reply you'd like to use) and practise using your answer.

KEEP IT SHORT & SIMPLE

Many of the books on networking advocate specific advice such as introductions of '10 words or less' or 'no more than two sentences'. However, although keeping it short is important, it is more critical that you are:

- **Clear** - use common words, no jargon
- **Concise** - use short words and sentences
- **Personable** - use engaging, friendly and warm words
- **Interest generating** - say something different or distinctive

You typically only have about 5–10 seconds to cover these four criteria, but this realistically gives you up to twenty words to use.

1: LEARNING STAGE

INTRODUCE YOURSELF

Specific introductions will be very much up to the individual style and personality. However, once again, this is an opportunity to stretch yourself to the edge of your comfort zone and present yourself as positively as you can. A simple example that meets all the above criteria might therefore be:

"Hello, my name is Christine Wheeler. I spend my time designing and running interactive booklets on networking."

Note that this has to cover what you do in practical terms and not just your name and job title.

Perhaps a more forthright example might be:

"Hello, my name is John Wright. I produce TV screen advertisements from script to screen and everything in between the two."

NOTES

THE INVESTING STAGE

2: INVESTING STAGE

INTRODUCTION

The Investing Stage simply involves each person in making deposits (or an investment) of time and energy, into building high quality relationships with their contacts.

To do this, every individual needs the right image and attitude and the patience to build trust over the long-term.

ESTABLISH THE RIGHT IMAGE

In the aim to be better at networking, you have learnt more about yourself, and thought a little about where to make a start. Now is the time to invest in making high-quality contacts, which starts with your own projected image. In this case, your image means how seriously your efforts to network are regarded by others, and how professional and organised you are seen to be.

Developing an organised and professional approach will partly depend on the individual and his or her specific networking goals. There is no uniform approach to take. However, one common (and often overlooked) image feature for every effective networker is the business or calling card (the summary information about yourself you choose to give to others).

CALLING CARD

Although there are no *hard* facts on the subject, it is estimated that 90% of people do not have a calling card at all. In fact, the estimated breakdown looks as follows:

- 90% of people have no calling card whatsoever

Of the 10% that do have a calling card:

- 25% have an informative card
- 35% have cards showing only name, address and phone number
- 40% have cards with out-of-date or incorrect information

This means that only 2.5 % of people have a card that is up to date, accurate and gives a reasonably full picture of who they are and what they do. (We will look at what a 'full picture' looks like in due course.)

ALWAYS CARRY YOUR CALLING CARDS

Having no calling card (or one that is inaccurate or short on detail) is a major inhibitor if you want to network successfully. Even a supply of blank cards is better than none at all, as you can't possibly expect people to remember everything that you tell them. Nor do you want constantly to write down names, phone numbers and any other information, in long hand, every time you meet someone.

The design of your calling card can vary enormously in style and look. However, it should be easy to read and include a minimum of name, address and daytime phone numbers. However, if appropriate, include fax number, e-mail address, mobile and home phone numbers.

FOCUS ON YOUR SKILLS NOT YOUR JOB

You'll notice that a job title is deliberately not included in the list. Although in principle there is nothing wrong with including it, it is much more useful to use the space under your name to describe what you do in a precise and concise way that is meaningful to anybody that you meet. Words like *designer of roads and bridges* or *seller of land and property* are much better than *engineer* or *sales consultant*.

Don't forget this is the information that helps others to know what skills you have or what you might offer. Hence, *secretary,* for example, is unlikely to be useful in itself but *expert in word processing and desktop publishing* says a lot more.

2: INVESTING STAGE

BUILD UP A CLEAR PICTURE

If you are going to network frequently, remembering all the data you collect can become quite a challenge (and an almost impossible one over time). As a result, you need to adopt an effective tracking system of some sort.

A tracking system doesn't have to be a sophisticated affair, but does need to record who you meet and what you learn about people.

One simple way to record information (for later filing or follow-up) is to use the calling cards you are given to note some extra details on the back. This could be:

● Something visual about the person
● The date/time/function when you met
● Who introduced you
● Topic of conversation
● Follow-up action, etc

BUILD RELATIONSHIPS, NOT CARD COLLECTIONS

In handing over your own calling cards, and in collecting those of other people, **your ultimate aim is to build relationships, not stacks of cards.** Your goal is therefore to create a good impression with the prospects you meet and to hand over (or collect) a calling card in a spirit of warmth, openness and co-operation (not as a trophy from the meeting). This means developing a confident way of reacting with people you meet, so that you present yourself as genuine in offering your thoughts, ideas or advice and leave an impression of what is often called an *abundance mentality*.

An *abundance mentality* is an attitude that there are more opportunities available than time or people to take advantage of them. We can therefore benefit from more of them together than we can apart. This means that you should be happy to hand over your business card, and happy to receive one (even though some people may decide that they don't want to bother – their loss rather than yours, of course).

BUILD THE RELATIONSHIP

By now, it should have become clear that **effective networking is more about what you can offer than what you may get from meeting with other people**. In basic terms, this means concentrating on creating a relationship in which useful information is exchanged every time (even if the first contact doesn't lead to any follow-up whatsoever).

A relationship is best built by creating and leaving a highly positive, courteous and professional impression on every person you talk to, and by always listening attentively to what they have to say to you.

2: INVESTING STAGE

DEVELOP YOUR LISTENING SKILLS

Developing the capacity to listen well is one of the best ways to find networking success quickly. This is because:

1. Many people are so busy telling other people what they do, want, are interested in, that they forget to listen to the other person properly, if at all.

2. In order to learn the right 'to ask for a referral and a favour' you have to learn what other people might find valuable first – you can only really do this *by listening attentively.*

As a rule, in all networking conversations, it is better to listen far more than you talk. **Successful networkers listen two to three times more than they talk**. Listening attentively is an art, and needs more time to discuss it fully than we can spend in this book. However, if you make good eye contact, show positive interest and don't interrupt, you will quickly elicit a lot of information and help people to feel warm towards you.

ASK GOOD QUESTIONS

Because you can't listen endlessly, or 100% of the time, one of the other skills closely connected with good listening is the ability to ask questions – but you do need to be careful. Questions can easily become intrusive and too direct when you meet with a stranger or someone you don't know well.

Good questions should probe your contact gently, and in a way that elicits information that can assist you to offer helpful thoughts and responses to what you hear.

Good questioners will use their questions to ask about the contact (and not ask questions that further their own interests). **The key is to establish empathy as quickly and as genuinely as you can.** This is usually best done by maintaining an open mind, allowing the other person to get their full message across and appreciating the feelings and the words being communicated.

MATCH YOUR WORDS WITH ACTIONS

In the effort to invest in long-term, high-quality relationships, one of the key ways in which to leave a positive impression upon a contact is to ensure that your actions match your words. In other words, your follow-up actions should be fast, decisive and consistent with what you promise.

For example, in a conversation with a network contact, you may suggest that you know somebody who could be of help or assistance and that you'll call them. If you make this kind of promise, call the person and then call back your contact to say you've done what you promised. This shows high levels of commitment and even goes beyond what they might have expected.

DO NOT MAKE RASH PROMISES

The habit of under-promising but over-delivery is likely to win you many friends (the reverse being the more usual experience for many people).

Usually, we genuinely want to do our best and believe that we can meet the commitments that we make. However, in our attempt to please someone in the short term, we sometimes compromise the longer term by ignoring the fact that we may run into difficulties, delays or obstacles. This very *natural* tendency will therefore only change through a focused effort.

NOTES

THE NURTURING STAGE

3: NURTURING STAGE

INTRODUCTION

Having developed network 'suspects' into live contacts, the Nurturing Stage involves the effective networker in building or nurturing the relationship with individuals.

This generally entails finding niche ways to offer your support and help, and maintaining a more systematic and regular approach to networking.

NICHE CHANNELS & OPPORTUNITIES

You may feel that once you have made contacts with people, started collecting a lot of calling cards and thereby increased considerably the number of people that you know, the hard part of more effective networking is complete. Although it is true that getting started is often the most difficult part of the journey, successful networking only really begins once you have a wide range of contacts to *nurture*.

Nurturing means finding ways to offer support to your network contacts. This can be described as:

'How well you create a mutual spirit of giving and sharing information'

LOOK FOR UNUSUAL OPPORTUNITIES

A large part of the process of nurturing your contacts is doing so in unusual ways. This is not because conventional ways of contact and follow-up don't work, but because this is the commonplace or popular way to do so. In other words, everybody is doing it. As a result, a contact may expect a follow-up call, letter, or 'thank you for your time' note (don't stop doing this if it works for you or for your contacts).

The way to nurture your contacts differently can be to focus on people's special or non-mainstream needs, challenges or potential problem areas. Let's look at a simple example to illustrate this.

3: NURTURING STAGE

FROM GENERAL TO SPECIFIC

You meet a contact who runs her own commercial enterprise (let's say selling second-hand musical instruments). She shares a range of comments about the pleasures and frustrations of being in a small business (cashflow, getting paid on time by customers, seasonality of trade, slow stock-turns, etc).

In listening to such contacts, the challenge is to separate what are general points (or conversational small talk) from specific points that are causing frustration or are issues yet to be solved.

Our second-hand instrument seller may want to offer new services, like playing tuition for instance, and may mention this in passing. This provides the opportunity to think about those people you might know with musical/interest and talent who might be useful to facilitate a connection.

3: NURTURING STAGE

LONG-TERM CONTACTS & REFERRALS

Effective networking is not an occasional, accidental or random process, and considerable personal organisation is therefore necessary. However, if you want to nurture your contacts to turn them into strong *advocates* and network *partners*, you will need to become even more systematic about your efforts and follow-up in general.

After you have been involving yourself in networking for even a few short weeks, you should have a lot of calling cards and other information. If this information sits randomly on a desk, or in piles or collected together in clips or rubber bands, you are not going to be either efficient or effective in following up properly (or, in some cases, at all!).

3: NURTURING STAGE

BE SYSTEMATIC AS A DAILY HABIT

First and foremost, feeding information into a system needs to be a daily habit (like cleaning your teeth at night). Habits form when you do something long enough for it to become a subconscious act. As a result, you need to make a commitment to filing or keying data into a computer religiously for at least several weeks.

Once you have developed your more systematic way of filing the cards, paper and other pieces of data, you can then start to think about how to organise everything to make the job of following up as easy as possible.

Although there is a range of professional and reasonably inexpensive 'contact management' software packages now available, even a simple *bring forward* manual system, rolodex or day journal will do the job very effectively.

DIARY EVERYTHING YOU WANT TO REMEMBER

Whatever *system* you use, the key organisational requirement is the same. When you meet someone new that you'd like to talk to again, or connect with somebody or something, diary it immediately (at least on the same day) even if the follow-up is to be one, three or six months later. This will give you a natural daily or weekly *to do* list to which you can add your other tasks or priorities.

Your list will also give you the opportunity to tick or cross off items that you have followed up successfully (or at least allow you to add forward actions that take your relationships to the next level).

3: NURTURING STAGE

USE YOUR SYSTEM TO FOLLOW UP

Once you have a system in place, the task of using it should become simple. For example, highly-experienced networkers will often use software to bring up their daily contacts and the notes from the last time they talked. Their system prompts them with other useful information like contact birthdays, anniversaries, etc. This helps to ensure that potentially important information is not forgotten or does not 'slip through the cracks'.

Experienced networkers also often make other means of following up easy for themselves by pre-printing personal stationery and thank you notes. They have any summary business information or promotional material to hand, keep stamped envelopes ready, and so on.

All this means **more professional and fast follow-ups** – something that almost inevitably impresses people.

3: NURTURING STAGE

PROCESS OF DISCOVERY

You don't have to be a sophisticated networker using the latest software to get good follow-up results. The most critical task is to make sure that you keep good notes for yourself, file them in some way that is useful to you and **always, always follow through.** Letting good contacts go to waste by failing to call or losing their cards makes much of your effort redundant. To quote Robyn Henderson again:

'You do not know what the (contact) opportunity will be, until you take the time to pursue it and discover what is there.'

This process of discovery is important for you and the other person, in as much as it promptly helps to establish whether the contact can be useful to either party (and if it can't or is unlikely, you can say so quickly and move on). The sort of questions that help in the process of discovery are shown on the next page.

3: NURTURING STAGE

QUESTIONS TO LEAD TO NEW CONTACTS

1. Who do you know who ......?
2. Where would you go if you wanted to ....?
3. What would you do in my situation?
4. Do you know of any paths that I could follow?
5. How would you proceed in taking the next steps?
6. What sort of people do you think could help me?
7. What do you recommend/advise ....?
8. Who do you know who is well connected/knows a lot of people?
9. What do you find are the best avenues to find someone to..?
10. Do you have a useful contact that I could call?

3: NURTURING STAGE

BE SEEN & GET KNOWN

Being seen and getting known simply means taking as many opportunities as you can to meet with people socially. Whilst a certain amount of networking can be done over the telephone, for the most part this means getting out and about and socialising in meetings, talks, societies, associations, clubs, etc.

As we said earlier, not every individual relishes high levels of social involvement in terms of their personal comfort. However, we are not suggesting that everyone needs to become the *life and soul* of the party or a centre of attraction in every social event that they attend.

Social involvement merely suggests that you attend social gatherings regularly and actively look to meet a few people to help progressively build your network.

3: NURTURING STAGE

EVERYONE IS IN THE SAME BOAT!

Despite the fact that you may not want to attend a social gathering or to network whilst you are there, don't forget, many people will feel the same way as you do. They will therefore naturally be grateful to anyone who has even a little confidence to take the conversational lead.

Remember, you are also there to offer and give, not to see what you can get.

As a result, there is little better for good networking opportunities than a group of people meeting together for almost any reason.

LOOK FOR INTERESTING EVENTS

Apart from clubs, associations and meetings in areas of direct interest to you, there is also a range of meetings specifically designed for networking purposes as a primary aim, or at least a strong secondary aim.

For instance, conferences, seminars, presentations and breakfast briefings may have a speaker or two to talk on a topic, but the rest of the meeting is often given over to lots of deliberate networking and calling card exchange.

Such events and meetings are promoted or advertised in a range of ways these days. You just need to be alert and on the lookout and get yourself along. If they really don't exist, **you could even consider starting up your own networking club.**

MAKE THE EFFORT TO ATTEND

Outside general social gatherings, most individuals start to network (or want to network more) for a range of personal reasons and to further their personal interests. Whatever these interests may be, there are often others who share them and hold their own get-togethers and events.

Unfortunately, many people who join chambers of commerce, clubs, societies, interest groups, etc, (even having paid a fee) attend no meetings, or perhaps just one in a whole year. This will do little to help with your networking efforts.

Even if a meeting is disappointing, it still represents an opportunity to connect with one or more people who in turn can connect you with people they know (who may prove to be very useful and interesting to you). As a result, if you join an interest club of any sort, it is worth attending the social events regularly. This may take some effort at the outset, but a good networker will stick to the task.

TAKE AN ACTIVE PART IN THE GROUP

It is possible to go well beyond being a relatively passive member of a club or interest group. You can take an active part in shaping what is said and done in the club's affairs. You can help to make it more lively and interesting, to attract more people or increase its influence and capacity to be a networking *hub*.

You could go even further in taking an active part by giving talks or presentations of your own or even writing letters or articles, if you feel so inclined. This will significantly lift your overall profile and be an excellent base upon which to build the quality of your own network. **This is not for everyone, but great if you have the confidence.**

THE NETWORKING 'SPIRAL' EFFECT

Although this networking change is a long-term and progressive one, it is likely to represent a significant shift in the way that you are perceived.

When you are perceived to be an effective networker, people will be drawn to you and beat a path to your door. This will not only be to ask for your help and assistance, but to offer opportunities to you first because people are confident that you will follow through and are likely to reciprocate. This tends to have a positive upward spiral effect:

more opportunities, larger network etc.

more well-known

more leads

more contacts

known to be a well-connected person

79

NOTES

THE KEEPING STAGE

4: KEEPING STAGE

INTRODUCTION

The last stage in networking entails consolidating your efforts in all the earlier stages and maintaining your overall momentum.

The Keeping Stage involves making sure that you are continually seen and that you become widely known. It also involves listening, and learning to become an excellent listener. This is where high levels of persistence and efforts to keep going are often necessary (in order to reap the long-term rewards).

LISTENING & LEARNING

It is likely to have become more obvious by now that **effective networking is only a systematic way to relate positively to people in the world around you.** In this sense, it is inevitably not only a lifelong journey, but one in which **you never truly stop listening and learning, so as to improve and grow personally.**

Good networking is also built on a foundation of valuing yourself (what we talked about as high self-esteem) and valuing others. This means believing in working with and through people to achieve the best results. It also means giving of yourself, without necessarily having a direct incentive to do so.

The underlying principle behind much of what we have said to this point has been our capacity to *tune in* to the needs of other people, in order to help them to achieve their goals or aspirations. For effective networking, there are three ways that this can be done. Let's look at each in turn.

1. DEVELOP LISTENING CHANNELS

Even if you are the most active, social and skilful networker in the world, there is a limit to the number of people you can meet or talk to. Hence, you will connect with most people by reaching *suspects* and *prospects* indirectly through others, or by your efforts to be visible to larger groups of people (making presentations, giving talks, writing for a wider audience, etc).

These indirect contacts therefore, become your *outposts* or *listening ears* for new potential connections. You therefore have to ensure that they know and understand the range of ways in which they can channel information deemed to be of interest to you.

At a practical level, this may be by phone, fax, e-mail, etc. However, it also means alerting your network advocates and partners to subjects and areas that are of interest to you and demonstrating a responsive openness to being called upon.

2. LISTENING FOR SUCCESS

It is an easy mistake to believe that networking is merely about having a lot of conversations or connections with as many people as you can. Unfortunately, we all engage in thousands of conversations every year, with only a handful truly qualifying as real networking.

This is simply because we do not ask questions to elicit information of value and interest most of the time, *and* **we often fail to listen carefully enough to what we are told.**

3. ACTIVE LISTENING MAKES THE DIFFERENCE

Active listening (or paying close attention through watching the other person and concentrating) does not take any more time than **not** doing so, and can reap the benefit of frequently revealing a connecting opportunity.

Experienced networkers will tell you that they glean networking opportunity information in one out of every two conversations that they have.

For us *ordinary mortals* it is nearer one in twenty, or ten times less effective! The difference is their capacity to listen actively for the possibilities and not drift away or dismiss the conversation as *boring, shallow, small talk, irrelevant,* etc.

ENCOURAGE CONTACTS TO TALK

It is worth repeating: networking is often about getting others to talk, **not** talking yourself. If you try this for real, the more you keep quiet and let the other person do the talking, the more they are likely to enjoy the conversation and find **you** interesting.

More importantly, the more a contact talks, the more you are likely to find out what issues are important for them and where their mind or their thinking may be focused. This can help to reveal challenges and issues that can help you to be supportive.

BE PERSISTENT

Most people understand and agree with the concept of persistence at a shallow level, but do not necessarily really comprehend its full implications. Persistence means being:

- Assiduous
- Constant
- Determined
- Dogged
- Enduring
- Fixed
- Immovable
- Incessant
- Indefatigable
- Obdurate
- Persevering
- Resolute
- Steadfast
- Stubborn
- Tenacious
- Tireless
- Unflagging
- Unrelenting

BEING HALF-HEARTED WILL GET YOU NOWHERE

Really successful networking is all of these things and therefore cannot be viewed as temporary, occasional, periodic or half-hearted, or anything else that is anything other than persistent.

Persistence is critical if you want to help yourself and others to network well over a period of time. This might be easier said than done, but unless you commit to persisting in this way, you may well become quickly frustrated and disappointed with your networking efforts.

MAINTAIN THE MOMENTUM: 1

Assuming that you have succeeded in building up a reasonably wide range of contacts in your early efforts, there are three specific actions that you can take to keep the momentum going.

1: Vary the method

You can maintain your contact partners by varying the means and methods that you use to communicate with them.

In addition to phone calls, you can drop people an e-mail, send a letter, note or card, invite them to a meeting or event, or plan to chat informally at a place or a time that will be convenient.

This variety will help your systematic attempts to keep in touch stay fresh and new.

MAINTAIN THE MOMENTUM: 2

2: Avoid a 'burn and churn' mentality

One of the enemies of networking persistence is becoming distracted by other events, priorities or activities which prevent you from maintaining contact.

In such circumstances, it is easy to adopt a 'burn and churn' mentality. This means that you take the view that it doesn't matter if you lose contact. There are plenty more *out there* that you can meet. Not only does this waste your time but the time of your contacts, and may quickly build you the kind of networking reputation that you don't want.

MAINTAIN THE MOMENTUM: 3

3: Keep your information current

Having invested time and energy in building up your contacts, you will need a lot of persistence to keep track of them, and keep the relationships growing.

Unfortunately, people do not stay still. They move house, change jobs, change contact numbers, adopt different interests, and many other things that can make your well-organised data quickly out of date, or even entirely redundant.

Some contacts are worth tracking and moving with. In other cases, it may be wiser to *edit* your contact system by accepting that a link has been broken. Your ultimate task is to do this as intelligently as you can.

SUMMARY

SUMMARY

This book has suggested that effective networking is achieved through deploying a four step model of:

❏ **Learning**   - about the needs of ourselves and others
❏ **Investing** - in making strong contacts with people
❏ **Nurturing** - deeper relationships
❏ **Keeping**   - the momentum going

As we have seen, this is not to say that networking is easy to define or practise, and we may spend a lifetime in trying to do it well.

SUMMARY

SEVEN NETWORKING 'COMPETENCIES'

During the course of this book, we have progressively described seven key 'competencies' needed for effective networking. These are:

1. Temperament/disposition
How well do you operate on an open, give and take basis with family, friends, colleagues and new contacts around you?

2. Strategising ability
How effectively do you think about the opportunities to network or build relationships and plan to take action?

3. Organisational skills
How effectively do you organise yourself and the information you gather about people you meet, so that you follow up efficiently and minimise wasted effort?

4. Nurturing ability
How well do you create a spirit of mutual giving and sharing of information?

SEVEN NETWORKING 'COMPETENCIES'

5. Communication skills
How effectively do you give and receive from your network in order to establish efficient communication channels?

6. Social involvement
How much do you involve yourself in social gatherings of all types to keep your network *fresh* and *alive?*

7. Persistence
With how much tenacity do you develop your personal network and drive hard towards better outcomes through people?

This is a difficult suite of skills to perfect. However, we can also see how beneficial the rewards can be for those that try.

Good luck with your efforts and for those of you ready to start immediately, read the final list of networking do's and don'ts as a final check.

NETWORKING DO'S

- ✔ Ask others for help
- ✔ Be friendly, warm and sincere
- ✔ Be persistent in following up and following through
- ✔ Focus carefully on learning people's names
- ✔ Be helpful to others even if there is no immediate or direct benefit to you
- ✔ Stay in touch regularly and systematically
- ✔ Always carry calling cards
- ✔ Get known as being *well-connected* (and a valuable resource for others)
- ✔ Sit next to strangers at events (not alone or with people you know)
- ✔ Keep networking even when you think you can stop

NETWORKING DON'TS

✗ Don't be impatient. Results and benefits can come when you least expect them and often take time

✗ Don't lose sight of your ultimate goal or objective

✗ Don't expect too much of others

✗ Don't have hidden agendas (not being up-front and straightforward with other people)

✗ Don't be insensitive to value, belief and cultural differences

✗ Don't fail to follow through when you find or are given leads

✗ Don't contact people only when you need something

✗ Don't go for quantity over quality in your relationships

✗ Don't try to do too much and spread yourself too thinly

✗ Don't try to network in a way that doesn't fit your style

SUMMARY

REFERENCES

The following books would provide useful reading for any individual wishing to learn more about networking and relationship building.

'The power of networking', Sandy Vilas and Donna Fisher, Thorsons, 1996

'How to master networking', Robyn Henderson, Prentice Hall, 1997

'Effective networking for professional success', Rupert Hart, Kogan Page, 1996

'Networking for everyone', L Michelle Tillier, JISworks, 1998

'Breakthrough networking - building relationships that last', Lillian Bjorseth, Duoforce, 1996

'Is your "net" working', Anne Boe and Bettie Youngs, John Wiley, 1989

The Networking Pocketbook is one is a series of Management Pocketbooks.
For more details and extra copies, complete the order form on the final page and return to Management Pocketbooks Ltd.

THE MANAGEMENT POCKETBOOK SERIES

Pocketbooks

Appraisals
Assertiveness
Balance Sheet
Business Planning
Business Writing
Call Centre Customer Care
Career Transition
Challengers
Coaching
Communicator's
Competencies
Controlling Absenteeism
Creative Manager's
C.R.M.
Cross-cultural Business
Cultural Gaffes
Customer Service
Decision-making
Developing People
Discipline
Diversity
E-commerce
Emotional Intelligence
Employment Law

Empowerment
Energy and Well-being
Facilitator's
Flexible Workplace
Handling Complaints
Icebreakers
Impact & Presence
Improving Efficiency
Improving Profitability
Induction
Influencing
International Trade
Interviewer's
I.T. Trainer's
Key Account Manager's
Leadership
Learner's
Manager's
Managing Budgets
Managing Cashflow
Managing Change
Managing Recruitment
Managing Upwards
Managing Your Appraisal

Marketing
Meetings
Mentoring
Motivation
Negotiator's
Networking
NLP
Openers & Closers
People Manager's
Performance Management
Personal Success
Positive Mental Attitude
Presentations
Problem Behaviour
Problem Solving
Project Management
Quality
Resolving Conflict
Sales Excellence
Salesperson's
Self-managed Development
Starting In Management
Strategy
Stress

Succeeding at Interviews
Teamworking
Telephone Skills
Telesales
Thinker's
Time Management
Trainer Standards
Trainer's
Training Evaluation
Training Needs Analysis
Vocal Skills

Pocketsquares

Great Training Robbery
Hook Your Audience

Pocketfiles

Trainer's Blue Pocketfile of
Ready-to-use Activities

Trainer's Green Pocketfile of
Ready-to-use Activities

Trainer's Red Pocketfile of
Ready-to-use Activities

26.5.05

About the Author

Jon Warner has spent over 20 years as a manager in a number of major multi-national companies in the United Kingdom, Europe, the United States of America and Australia. This experience has included time as a senior staff manager in human resources and a number of line roles with responsibility for large groups of people. During the last 5 years Jon has been involved in broad-ranging organisational consultancy. This consulting has taken him into a number of major organisations such as Mobil Oil, the National Bank, BTR, Qantas, Gas and Fuel, United Energy, Air Products and Chemicals, General Motors and Barclays Bank. Jon is also Managing Director of Team Publications Limited, based in Australia, an international training and publishing company committed to bringing practical and fun-to-use learning material to the market. Jon has written and published a wide range of management books, manuals and diagnostic instruments (including one on networking).

Jon can be contacted at the following addresses:
UK: PO Box 28, Camarthen, Dyfed, Wales. Tel: +44 (0)1267 281661 Fax: +44 (0)1267 281315
Australia: Building 2, 175 Varsity Parade, Gold Coast, Queensland, Australia.
Tel. +617 5553 6099   Fax. +617 5580 8928

Published by: Management Pocketbooks Ltd.
                Laurel House, Station Approach, Alresford, Hants SO24 9JH, U.K.
                Tel: +44 (0)1962 735573 Fax: +44 (0)1962 733637
                E-mail: sales@pocketbook.co.uk Website: www.pocketbook.co.uk

Design, typesetting and graphics by **efex ltd**   Printed in U.K.   ISBN 1 870471 80 6

ORDER FORM

	No. copies

Your details

Name _____

Position _____

Company _____

Address _____

_____

_____

Telephone _____

Fax _____

E-mail _____

VAT No. (EC companies) _____

Your Order Ref _____

Please send me:

	No. copies
The Networking _____ Pocketbook	☐
The _____ Pocketbook	☐
The _____ Pocketbook	☐
The _____ Pocketbook	☐
The _____ Pocketbook	☐

Order by Post
MANAGEMENT POCKETBOOKS LTD
LAUREL HOUSE, STATION APPROACH, ALRESFORD,
HAMPSHIRE SO24 9JH UK

Order by Phone, Fax or Internet
Telephone: +44 (0)1962 735573
Facsimile: +44 (0)1962 733637
E-mail: sales@pocketbook.co.uk
Web: www.pocketbook.co.uk

Customers in USA should contact:
Stylus Publishing, LLC, 22883 Quicksilver Drive,
Sterling, VA 20166-2012
Telephone: 703 661 1581 or 800 232 0223
Facsimile: 703 661 1501 E-mail: styluspub@aol.com